FREDERICK WARNE

Published by the Penguin Group, 27 Wrights Lane, London W8 5'TZ, England
Penguin Books USA Inc., 375 Hudson Street, New York, New York 10014, USA
Penguin Books Australia Ltd, Ringwood, Victoria, Australia
Penguin Books Canada Ltd, 10 Alcorn Avenue, Toronto, Ontario, Canada M4V 3B2
Penguin Books (N.Z.) Ltd, 182-190 Wairau Road, Auckland 10, New Zealand

Penguin Books Ltd, Registered Offices: Harmondsworth, Middlesex, England

First published 1983 by Frederick Warne
This edition with new reproductions of Beatrix Potter's book illustrations first published 1987

Devised by Judy Taylor

From *Cecily Parsley's Nursery Rhymes*

ISBN 0 7232 3157 5

Printed and bound in Great Britain by William Clowes Limited, Beccles and London

MY FIRST YEAR

A Beatrix Potter Baby Book

From *Appley Dapply's Nursery Rhymes*

Devised by Judy Taylor

With new reproductions from the original illustrations

BY BEATRIX POTTER

F. WARNE & Co. ™

My Birth

My name is

....

I was born

On ....At ....(time)

Place ....

Doctor ....Midwife ....

I went home on ....

From *The Tale of Two Bad Mice*

My Birth

When I was born

I weighed ....

I measured ....

My eyes were...

My hair was ....

From *The Tale of Jeremy Fisher*

My birth was announced like this

(Stick down card or newspaper cutting)

My Family

From *The Tale of The Flopsy Bunnies*

Detail from *The Tale of Benjamin Bunny*

My parents

Mother ....

Father...

My grandparents

....

....

My Family

I have............brothers and..............sisters

....

....

....

We live at

....

....

Our pets are

From *The Tale of Jemima Puddle-Duck*

....

....

....

....

My Names

My full names

....

....

....

....

My names were chosen because

.... *(is my grandmother's/grand-*

father's/ .... name)

....

....

....

"Name?
Please?"

From *The Art of Beatrix Potter*

10

My Names

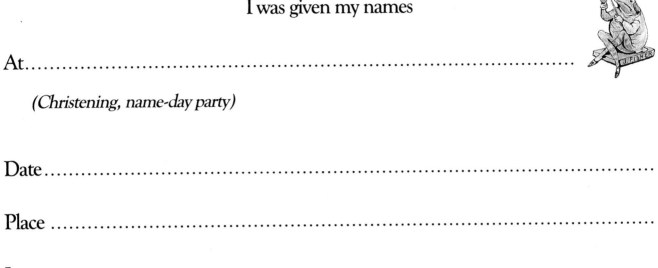

I was given my names

At..

(Christening, name-day party)

Date..

Place ....

I wore ....

Those who came

....

....

....

....

....

From *The Tailor of Gloucester*

My Progress

At one month

I weighed ....

And measured ....

At two months

....

At three months

....

At four months

....

At five months

....

At six months

....

At seven months

....

At eight months

....

From *The Tale of Ginger and Pickles*

At nine months

....

At ten months

....

At eleven months

....

At one year

....

My Progress

I have been immunized against

Type...   Date...

....

....

....

....

My illnesses

....

....

....

....

....

From *The Tale of Peter Rabbit*

My Progress

I ate my first real food on ....

It was ....

From *The Sly Old Cat*

I drank from a cup by myself on ....

In the cup was ....

My Progress

I was fully weaned on ....

My first complete meal was ....

....

The food I like best is ....

....

From *The Tale of Johnny Town-Mouse*

15

Important Landmarks

From *The Story of a Fierce Bad Rabbit*

I first focused my eyes *(date)* ....

Smiled ....

Rolled over ....

Slept through the night ....

Laughed out loud ....

Sat up ....

Important Landmarks

Moved from a cradle to a cot

....

Crawled...

Had my nails cut ....

Stood up ....

Took a step unaided ....

Had my hair cut ....

My first pair of shoes............................

Walked ....

Ran...

From *The Tale of Timmy Tiptoes*

I cut my teeth
(number the chart)

1 ....

2 ....

3 ....

4 ....

5 ....

6 ....

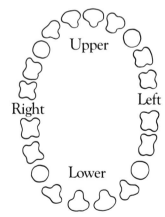

Upper

Right

Left

Lower

7 ....

8 ....

9 ....

10...................................

11...................................

12...................................

Important Landmarks

My first words

.... Date ....

....　...

....　...

....　...

....　...

....　...

From *The Story of Miss Moppet*

Important Landmarks

My first toys

.... Given to me by ....

....

....

....

....

My first clothes

....

....

....

....

Detail from *The Tale of Mrs. Tiggy-Winkle*

My first books

.... Given to me by ....

....

....

....

From *The Tale of Tom Kitten*

Tea with Granny, birthday parties, etc.

Date………………………………………… Place ……………………………………………

……………………………………………………………………………………………………

……………………………………………………………………………………………………

Date………………………………………… Place ……………………………………………

……………………………………………………………………………………………………

……………………………………………………………………………………………………

Outings

Date..Place ....

....

....

Date..Place ....

....

....

From *Peter Rabbit's Diary*

21

My First Christmas

December 25, 19

Where spent ....

....

The weather was ....

Other people there ....

....

....

....

From *The Tale of Two Bad Mice*

My presents

....

....

....

....

....

....

From *The Tale of Squirrel Nutkin*

My First Birthday

From *The Tale of Mrs. Tittlemouse*

Date ....

Where spent ....

....

Other people there ....

....

....

....

....

My presents

....

....

....

....

....

....

From *The Tale of The Pie and The Patty-pan*

My Photographs

From *The Tale of Pigling Bland*

My Photographs

From *The Tailor of Gloucester*

My Photographs

From *The Tale of Ginger and Pickles*

My Photographs

From *The Tale of Mr. Tod*

My Photographs

From *The Tale of Samuel Whiskers*

My Future

From *The Tale of Little Pig Robinson*

And off I venture into
My Second Year